Monographic Journals of the Near East *Afroasiatic Linguistics* 6/1 (December 1978)

THEORETICAL IMPLICATIONS OF CONSONANT SEQUENCE CONSTRAINTS IN ISRAELI HEBREW

by

Malachi Barkai
Tel Aviv University, Israel

Seven constraints on consonant sequences in Israeli Hebrew, which are the modern reflexes of older Semitic constraints, are discussed in relation to three levels: (i) as Morpheme Structure Conditions imposed on the underlying consonantal root morpheme; (ii) as Surface Phonetic Constraints imposed on the word regardless of morphemic content; (iii) as Morpheme Sensitive Surface Constraints, which as the name suggests, are placed on words, but are sensitive to morphemic structure and categorization. The third set of constraints has not been seriously considered in the recent literature, yet at least some of the seven different constraints must be regarded as morpheme-sensitive. The root level is seen to play little or no role in determining these constraints.

CONTENTS

1. INTRODUCTION 2

2. THE SEQUENTIAL CONSTRAINTS 3
 2.1. The identity constraint 4
  2.1.1. Root level 4
  2.1.2. As a surface phonetic constraint (SPC) 4
  2.1.3. As a morpheme-sensitive surface constraint (MSSC) 4
 2.2. The voicing constraint 6
  2.2.1. Root 6
  2.2.2. SPC 6
  2.2.3. MSSC 7
 2.3. The dental constraint 7
  2.3.1. Root 7
  2.3.2. SPC 7
  2.3.3. MSSC 8
 2.4. The sonorant constraint 8
  2.4.1. Root 8
  2.4.2. SPC 8
  2.4.3. MSSC 9
 2.5. The glottal constraint 9
  2.5.1. Root 9
  2.5.2. SPC 9
  2.5.3. MSSC 10

2.6. The labial constraint 10
2.6.1. Root 10
2.6.2. SPC 10
2.6.3. MSSC 10
2.7. The velar-glottal constraint 11
2.7.1. Root 11
2.7.2. SPC 11
2.7.3. MSSC 11

3. CONCLUSION 12

REFERENCES 13

> Were such things here, as we do speak about,
> Or have we eaten on the insane root
> That takes the reason prisoner?
> Macbeth, I, iii 83-5

1. INTRODUCTION[1]

It is widely accepted that one of the outstanding characteristics of the Semitic languages is their use of the consonantal root. The consonantal root, it has been held, carries the lexical or semantic meaning while, as far as the verbal system is concerned, the vowels indicate tense or aspect, i.e. they have a basically grammatical function (for discussion, see Ullendorff (1970)). The typical root is triconsonantal, though bi- and quadriconsonantal roots are not uncommon.

Greenberg (1950) in his well-known study of co-occurrence constraints on consonants analyzed triconsonantal roots as found in classical Arabic. He showed that there are various phonological constraints on which consonants can co-occur in first and second radical position (R_1 and R_2 respectively); as well as on R_2 and R_3 and even in some cases R_1 and R_3. For example, the non-labial sonorant consonants /r l d/ cannot co-occur within the same root. Thus, *ldr*, *rld*, *drl*, *dlr*, etc. are all unacceptable.

This study investigates sequential constraints synchronically, not in early Semitic, but in a spoken Semitic language, namely Israeli (or Modern) Hebrew (IH). The standard Ashkenazi (or European-derived) dialect of Hebrew is taken as the basis.

In section 2, after presentation of the consonantal phonemes of IH, seven sequential constraints will be tested as to the level in the grammar at which the proposed constraint is to be applied. In current phonological theory, there are two pervading schools of thought. In transformational generative phonology, as epitomized by the work, for example, of Halle (1959), Chomsky and Halle (1968), Schane (1968) sequential constraints are imposed on the underlying morphemes. In the case of this study, the relevant underlying morphemes are the consonantal roots. In natural generative phonology, e.g. Vennemann (1974), Hooper (1976), Hudson (1974), the proper level of application of sequential constraints is the phonetic level, and they are referred to as Surface Phonetic Constraints (SPC's). SPC's apply to the level of the surface word, the morpheme content of which is disregarded. SPC's as Shibatani writes, "represent true generalizations about the phonetic pattern of a language" (1973:88). SPC's are clearly related to pronounceability. We shall remark on this question when dealing with the Labial Constraint (see below, 2.7). SPC's have been couched in terms of the syllable (note Hooper (1976)). Since the sequential constraints in question often affect the coda of one syllable and the onset of the next, we shall, however, pursue the analysis ignoring the syllable.

Another possible approach which we shall maintain and support is that at least some morphemic information must be considered when applying constraints at the surface level. We shall refer to this proposition as morpheme-sensitive surface constraints. As far as we are aware, such a proposal has not been made explicitly, though the possibility has been broached by Bach in a personal communication cited by Clayton (1976:302, fn. 7).

To summarize: the viability of each constraint will be examined in detail in one of three ways. As

(i) a constraint imposed on the underlying root;

(ii) a surface phonetic constraint placed on words, which is insensitive to morphemic content;

(iii) a morpheme-sensitive surface constraint (henceforth MSSC) which examines the surface representation and is sensitive to morphemic information.

2. THE SEQUENTIAL CONSTRAINTS

The consonantal segments, both at the level of the root and at the surface level, are:

Labial:	/p b f v m/
Dental:	/t d s z/ and the voiceless affricate /c/
Palato-alveolar:	/š/
Velar:	/k g x/
Glottal:	/? h/
Non-labial sonorants:	/n l r/

The principal focus of attention will be the verbal root. We note that, in general, any three consonants may be combined to form a root, e.g. *šbr* 'break'; *rkb* 'ride'; *bdk* 'examine'; *stm* 'block'; *mnʔ* 'prevent'; *lkx* 'take', etc. However, as stated previously, certain sequential constraints apply. These constraints[1] will be discussed under the following seven rubrics:

i) the identity constraint (IC);

ii) the voicing constraint (VC);

iii) the dental constraint (DC);

iv) the sonorant constraint (SC);

v) the glottal constraint (GC);

vi) the labial constraint (LC);

vii) the velar-glottal constraint (VGC).

[1]The counterparts of these constraints can be found in Greenberg (1950), though they have been modified in varying degrees by historical change. Sequences not found but which have no plausible phonological reason for their absence, e.g. *vs*, are not considered.

2.1. THE IDENTITY CONSTRAINT

According to the IC, no two contiguous[2] consonants may be identical.

2.1.1. Root Level

It is well known that in Semitic R_2 and R_3 are very often identical (though not contiguous). In IH there are numerous examples, e.g. *šdd* 'rob', *svv* 'turn around', *hss* 'hesitate', *zmm* 'plot against', *pll* 'pray', etc. In Semitic, however, in R_1 and R_2 positions identity was forbidden, although recent formations indicate that this constraint should not be imposed at the root level in modern Hebrew. The new formations include *mmš* 'realize' and *mmn* 'finance'. An older form which constituted an exception to the constraint is *ddy* 'waddle'. The verb *ttʾ* 'sweep' has been reconstructed from *tʾtʾ*. The first glottal stop, however, never surfaces or gives any morphophonemic indication of its presence.

2.1.2. The IC as a Surface Phonetic Constraint

Following Shibatani (1973), we interpret the phonetic level throughout as referring to a level of careful formal speech. Predictable allophonic variation is not considered.

Identical consonants (i.e. geminate-like clusters) may arise at the contact of a root consonant and one belonging to an affix . Thus note:

(1) /hittame/ 'become unclean' (prefix *hit-*)

(2) /hittaher/ 'become clean' (prefix *hit-*)

(3) /šafâtti/ 'I judged' (suffix *-ti*)

(4) /risânnu/ 'we restrained' (suffix *-nu*)[3]

The four verbs referred to in 2.1.1, however, namely *mmš*, *mmn*, *ttʾ* and *ddy* never surface with juxtaposed consonants, since they all belong to verb class 2 (*pi'el*)[4] which in all its forms has an intervening non-deletable vowel between R_1 and R_2, e.g. *mimeš* 'he realized', *yemameš* 'he will realize', *memameš* 'realize' (pres.), *mimuš* 'realization'. Nevertheless, the existence of forms such as those represented by 1 through 4 prevents us from defining identity constraints as surface phonetic.

2.1.3. As a Morpheme-Sensitive Surface Constraint

In examples 1 through 4 a cluster of identical consonants straddles a morphemic break. *Hit-* is a reflexive prefix representing verb class 4 (*hitpa'el*); *-ti* 'I', *-ta* 'you' (masc.sing.), *-t* 'you' (fem.sing.), *-tem* 'you' (plur.), and *-nu* 'we' represent past tense pronominal suffixes. Thus, all verbs which have /t/ or /n/ as R_3 can have a surface form with a

---

[2] In IH, there is no mutual dependency between R_1 and R_3. All the constraints will therefore be discussed as applying either to R_1 and R_2 and/or to R_2 and R_3.

[3] Enumerated examples are given in their phonetic representation as defined, unless otherwise indicated by the use of traditional notations. Stress is final, unless explicitly shown.

[4] The phonological and morpho-syntactic ramifications of the verb class (*binyan*) system were discussed in Barkai (1975).

phonetically identical cluster. As there are in Hebrew no cases of identity at the surface level within the morpheme, we are led to suggest that IC must be considered as an MSSC.

This view is corroborated by a process which blocks spirantization of a post-vocalic velar stop into a fricative before a velar fricative. Thus:

(5) *katav* (verb class 1) 'he wrote' ~ *yixtov* (verb class 1) 'he will write', *nixtav* (verb class 7 - *nif'al*) 'it was written', *hixtiv* (verb class 5 - *hif'il*) 'he dictated', etc.

(6) *kêtem* 'a stain', *hixtim* (verb class 5) 'he stained'

From /hi+kxiš/ (verb class 5) 'he denied' or /hi+kxid/ (verb class 5) 'he destroyed' we would expect **hixxiš*, **hixxid* but instead the surface forms are *hikxiš*, *hikxid* without spirantization. It is true that not all /k/s spirantize (those derived historically from /q/ and written with a "qof" do not), but R_1 in *kxš* and *kxd* is historically derived from /k/, represented orthographically by "kaf" and does spirantize. In highly formal normative or learned speech, one hears *hixəxiš*, *hixəxid* — forms which also, of course, prevent identical consonants from being contiguous within a morpheme.

Another example of the avoidance of a cluster of identical consonants was brought to my attention by Bolozky (personal communication). From the noun form *xacocra* 'trumpet', the root *xccr* would be derived. All quadriliteral roots in IH are assigned to verb class 2 (*pi'el*), thus we would expect the canonic form **xiccer* (past) ~ **yexaccer* (fut.), etc. Instead there is a metathesis. The surface forms are in fact *xicrec* ~ *yexacrec*, etc. and the IC is observed. *xicrec*, too, is paralleled by a learned non-methathesized form which surfaces as *xicəcer* with a schwa epenthesis which also preserves the IC.

In all dialects, learned or vulgar, there is a rule which epenthesizes a lax mid front vowel /e/ between two identical consonants, provided the second consonant precedes a morpheme boundary (+):

e-epenthesis: $\phi \rightarrow e \ / \ C_1 \_\_\_ C_2 \ +$ [5]

(where $C_1 = C_2$ in all features, though the value for voicing may vary—note further the discussion on VC).

Feeding this rule is a process whereby the second stem vowel in the verb is deleted when it precedes a suffix which has an initial stressed vowel:

Vowel Truncation: $V \rightarrow \phi \ / \ \_\_\_ \ C + \acute{V}$

Vowel truncation precedes epenthesis. Note the following examples:

(7) *šamar* (verb class 1) 'he kept' ~ *šamrú* (/šamar+u/) 'they kept'

(8) *kibes* (verb class 2) 'he laundered' ~ *kibsá* (/kibes+a/) 'she laundered'

(9) *yexabes* (verb class 2) 'he will launder' ~ *yexabsú* (/ye+kabes+u/) 'they will launder, etc.

---

[5]Examples 1 through 4 indicate that epenthesis does not apply inter-morphemically. Avoidance of forms such as *hixəxiš*, *xicəcer* in everyday speech indicates further that the rule does not apply only intra-morphemically. There are no exceptions to the rule as postulated.

Where $C_2 = C_3$ e-epenthesis applies:

(10) *šadad* ~ *šadedu* 'robbed'

(11) *yehalel* ~ *yehalelu* 'praise', etc.[6]

The effect of epenthesis is, of course, to prevent the identical consonants from clustering as a result of vowel truncation. As stated previously, epenthesis does not normally occur at all inter-morphemically where identical clusters may arise. In short, what is relevant is the morpheme structure of the surface word.

2.2. THE VOICING CONSTRAINT

This forbids a sequence of two obstruents which differ only in voicing.

2.2.1. Root.

There are at least three examples which would violate the VC if it were imposed at this level: *ʔtd* 'be destined to', *tdrx* 'guide', *tdlk* 'fuel'. All three examples indicate the sequence *td*; the reverse is not found, nor are %*pb*, %*kg*, %*fv* or %*sz* (% indicates the converse sequence). This might suggest that the constraint be allowed to operate at the level of the root with exclusion of the sequence *td*. However, when taking an overall view of these seven constraints, it will be noticed that the root is not the most apposite level at which to place them. As will be seen from the following discussion on SPC's and MSSC's, a broad generalization may be made.

2.2.2. SPC

Examples (1) and (2) cited in the discussion on the IC contain the reflexive prefix /hit/. When /t/ precedes a root with initial /d/ it will almost certainly undergo regressive voicing assimilation. Thus:

(12) /hit+darder/ → *hiddarder* (with subsequent degemination in more casual speech) 'deteriorated'

However, where /d/ is R_3 and precedes a suffix with initial /t/, voicing assimilation may be much more readily suppressed (in general voicing assimilation is optional in IH). The following forms certainly cannot be ruled out from the phonetic representation:

(13) *lamádti* 'I learned'

(14) *limádta* 'you taught', etc.

There are, however, dialect differences with regard to these forms; in some dialects epenthesis applies (also when R_3 = /t/, e.g. *šafáteti* 'I judged', note example 3):

(15) *lamádeti* 'I learned'

(16) *limádeti* 'I taught'

---

[6]An alternative approach is for vowel truncation to apply only between non-identical consonants, with a rule which specifies the underlying second stem vowel as /e/ in the environment of identical consonants. However, noun patterns of the form /CaCC+an/, e.g. *savlan* 'a patient person', *rakdan* 'a dancer', where there is no evidence of an underlying vowel between R_2 and R_3, surface with intervening [e] when there is identity, e.g. *xatetan* 'a busybody', *lakekan* 'a flatterer', etc. (see also Cole (1973)).

The same difference is found where /d/ precedes the idiosyncratic third person feminine singular past tense marker /t/ found in verbs with (historically at least) /y/ as R_3, e.g.

(17) /bad+t+a/ *badta* or *badeta* 'she lied'

These facts indicate a dialect division. When epenthesis does not apply, VC cannot be regarded as a constraint on the surface word (unless we were explicitly to exclude dental stop clusters from the constraint). In dialects where epenthesis obligatorily applies, however, VC may be regarded as an SPC.

2.2.3. MSSC

In all the examples of two obstruents which differ only in voicing discussed in the previous section, the two consonants in question are on different sides of a morpheme boundary. One is part of a root, the other is part of an inflected morpheme.

Within the root morpheme (no inflectional morpheme contains a consonant cluster), the verbs *ᵓtd*, *tdrx* and *tdlk* given above as counter-examples to the constraint at the root level, exhibit surface vowels in all forms between the relevant consonants. Thus *ᵓtd* is assigned to verb class 4 (*hitpa'el*). The application of vowel truncation would lead to a surface form **hitᵓatda*. However, epenthesis applies resulting in the surface form *hit(ᵓ)ateda*.

tdrx and *tdlk*, being quadriliteral roots are assigned to verb class 2 (*pi'el*). In this verb class, it will be recalled, a surface vowel representing a tense morpheme always intervenes between R_1 and R_2.

From this, we see that, in all dialects of IH, the VC is applicable within the morpheme. Furthermore, since there are no counter-examples involving non-dental plosives, it may be imposed as a general constraint on all obstruent sequences.

2.3. THE DENTAL CONSTRAINT

It prevents the sequence of a dental stop followed by a dental sibilant. The reverse order is commonly found, at all levels in the language, e.g. *str*: *histir* 'conceal', *ctt*: *citet* 'quote', *cdd*: *cided* 'side with', etc.

2.3.1. Root

Several verbs would violate the constraint if it were imposed at this level: *tss* 'ferment', *ntc* 'smash', *tsbx* 'have a complex', *tzmr* 'orchestrate', etc.

2.3.2. SPC

The verb form *tss* 'ferment' is assigned either to verb class 1 with intransitive meaning or to verb class 5 when used transitively. In either case, forms with no intervening vowel can arise, e.g. *yitsos* (verb class 1) 'it will ferment(int.)', *yatsis* (verb class 5) 'he will ferment(trans.)'. Similarly, from *ntc* (verb class 2) we have /nitec+a/ 'she smashed', which does not show epenthesis after application of vowel truncation: the surface form is *nitca*.

Nominalized forms[7] with the prefix /t/ are also counter-examples to an assumed DC:

(18) *tsumat* (*lev*) 'attention' (*lev* 'heart') from /t+sum+at/

(19) *tzuza* 'movement' from /t+zuz+a/, etc.

---

[7]Non-verbal forms are considered in relation to SPCs since morphological information is irrelevant.

2.3.3. MSSC

Since forms like *yitsos* and *nitcu* allow dental stop + dental sibilant sequences within the morpheme, the DC cannot be regarded as a viable constraint in IH at this level (or, as we have seen, at any other).

This constraint once applied in Semitic in general and in Hebrew in particular but has now been lost. Its operation can still be discerned in the old and still productive rule of metathesis of the prefix-final /t/ of the reflexive form with a sibilant R_1 (before /z/ with accompanying voicing assimilation):

(20) /hit+cadek/ → *hictadek* 'justify oneself'

(21) /hit+salek/ → *histalek* 'leave; get out'

(22) /hit+zakek/ → *hizdakek* 'need'

While metathesis was no doubt once the reflection of a constraint which prevented dental stop-sibilant sequences in IH, though still operative, it is no longer a surface constraint.

2.4. THE SONORANT CONSTRAINT

It forbids sequences of the non-labial sonorant consonants /r l n/.

2.4.1. Root

Roots which violate this constraint include *grl* 'draw lots', *nrtk* 'sheathe', *rnn* 'gladden', *krn* 'radiate', *lnn* 'complain', *prns* 'support'.

2.4.2. SPC

Of the verbs cited above, *rnn* and *prns* have surface clusters which violate the constraint. Thus:

(23) *hirnin* (verb class 5) 'gladden'

(24) *pirnes* (verb class 2) 'support'

In the other verb forms a vowel always intervenes. *grl* and *krn* are both assigned to verb class 5 where the vowel, which is stressed throughout, is never deleted, e.g.

(25) *higríla* 'she drew lots'

(26) *hikrína* 'she radiated'

Somewhat less rarely used (at least verbally) is *krn* 'radiate' (intrans.) in verb class 1. When it is used epenthesis does not take place:

(27) *karna* 'she radiated'

All of these examples, it will be noted, contain an *rn* sequence; other combinations of sonorant consonants are not found.

However, as previously mentioned, an SPC is applied to any word in the language regardless of morphological information. Thus, the existence or absence of examples from non-verbal forms is of crucial importance. We note that all of the so-called forbidden sequences are found in non-verbal forms. Thus:

(28) lr: *milra* 'penultimate'

(29) rl: *ᵓorla* 'foreskin'

(30) ln: *kolnoʻa* 'cinema'

(31) nl: *benleᵓumi* 'inter (=*ben*)-national (*leumi*)

(32) nr: *kinrot* 'area near the Sea of Galilee'

(33) rn: *orne* 'pinetrees' (construct)

2.4.3. MSSC

If only the root morpheme or the surface word were recognized as being the proper levels of application of sequential constraints, we would not be able to make the necessary generalization that certain phonological natural classes cannot co-occur in verbal forms. SC, excluding *rn*, should then be regarded as a verb-constrained MSSC.[8]

2.5. THE GLOTTAL CONSTRAINT

It forbids a sequence of the two glottal obstruents: %ᵓ*h*.

2.5.1. Root

Within the root, there are at least two violations: *ᵓhv* 'love' and *ᵓhd* 'sympathize'. The reverse order, *hᵓ*, is not found.

2.5.2. SPC

The constraint as stated is much too narrow. In IH, no glottal can ever immediately precede any consonant. Either the glottal is deleted (examples 34-5), or a vowel is inserted between the glottal and the following consonant (examples 36-41):

(34) *karᵓa* 'she read', contrast *gamra* 'she finished'
karáti 'I read' *gamárti* 'I finished'

(35) *tamha* 'she was amazed'
tamánu 'we were amazed', contrast *gamárnu* 'we finished'

(36) *yaᵓaroz* (or *yeᵓeroz*) 'he will pack', contrast *yigmor* 'he will finish'

(37) (ᵓ)*ariza* 'packing', contrast *gmira* 'finishing'

---

[8]In IH, loan words are adapted into the verbal system, normally by rejection of the vowels and in the case of quadriliterals by assignment to verb class 2, thus: *telefon*, root *tlfn*; verb class 2 - *tilfen*; *hipnot*(ize), root - *hpnt*; verb class 2 - *hipnet*; etc. 'Flirt' should then have given root - *flrt*, verb class 2 - **filret* which would have led to a violation of the SC; instead the surface form is *flirtet*, thus the violation is avoided. This suggestive example was brought to my attention by Bolozky (personal communication).

(38) *yaharos* 'he will destroy'

(39) *harisa* 'destruction'

(40) *šaʾala* 'she asked' (note 27 above)

(41) *mahala* 'she mixed'

This constraint applies as an SPC anywhere within the word

2.5.3. MSSC

As GC is an SPC it follows that internal morphemic structure is irrelevant here.

2.6. THE LABIAL CONSTRAINT

As it formerly applied, it prevented a sequence of two labial consonants.

2.6.1. Root

ybm 'perform a levirate marriage', *gbv* 'pile', *lpf* 'entwine', *gpf* 'hug', etc. Some gaps may be found in the system, e.g. *fp*, *vb*, *vm*, etc. These are caused either by the very low frequency of /v/ or as a result of a highly complex spirantization process (see Barkai (1972) for some further discussion) which has resulted in segment constraints banning /f/ from word- (or root-) initial position and labial stops /p/ and /b/ from word- (or root-) final position. The gaps, however, are not systematic and need not be considered in detail. It is clear from the examples given that there is no constraint on labials at the root level that can be put in the form of a generalization.

2.6.2. SPC

The rule of epenthesis following vowel truncation applies where the distinction between the labials lies only in their continuancy value (stop-fricative)—note examples (42-3)—but not where the nasal consonant is involved (example 44).

(42) /lipef+a/ → *lipfa* → *lipefa* (??*lipfa*) 'she entwined'

(43) /gibev+a/ → *gibva* → *gibeva* (??*gibva*) 'she piled'

(44) /yibem+a/ → *yibma* (**yibema*) 'she underwent a levirate marriage'

Within nouns, labial obstruents cannot occur in sequences though L*m* or *m*L (where L is a labial obstruent) sequences are found:

(45) *pumpiya* 'grater'

(46) *gamba* 'pimento'

(47) *ʾambatya* 'bath'

(48) *sifme* 'moustaches' (construct)

2.6.3. MSSC

To regard LC as an SPC, however, appears to be justifiable only on observational grounds. If prefixes had terminated in a labial obstruent, say *hif* for reflexive *hit*, or suffixes had commenced with a labial, e.g. *bi* for *ti*, no process would have blocked sequences such as *hifparnes* (for actually occurring *hitparnes*) or *gandvbi* (for *gandvti*). In short, LC is potentially violable within words. To treat it as an SPC would have ranked it together with GC which, we have argued, is a genuine SPC. The essential difference is that glottal-consonant sequences cannot be pronounced. SPC's give information about pronounceability. A labial cluster, however, is quite pronounceable. If we treat the LC as an MSSC—where the relevant morpheme is basically the verb stem—then we need not be concerned about pronounceability, since information about the internal morphemic structure of a word is totally irrelevant as far as this factor is concerned.

Furthermore, we have positive evidence that morphemic information is required in considering the LC, since epenthesis, which serves to break up labial sequences, e.g. *gibeva*, *lipefa*, etc., applies within the stem.

One final comment on SPC's and MSSC's is that we might expect that at least certain types of SPC's are not violable in faster or more casual speech, whereas MSSC's may be. Restricting our remarks to the data discussed in this article, we note that the GC can never be violated. Although the epenthesized vowel (note examples 36-41) may be deleted in faster speech, so will the glottal obstruent, e.g. /ya+haros/ in faster speech may become *yaaros* or *yaros* (see Bolozky 1976) but never **yahros*. An MSSC, since it is not a constraint on pronunciation but tells us about the internal oraganization of morphemes, is subject to violation in faster or more casual speech. Thus *gibeva* or *lipefa* may well be reduced to *gibva*, *lipfa*, etc.

2.7. THE VELAR-GLOTTAL CONSTRAINT

This forbids a sequence of a velar fricative, i.e. the voiceless velar fricative /x/ which has no voiced counterpart, and the glottal fricative /h/, and vice versa.[9]

2.7.1. Root

There are no roots which violate this constraint. There is one potential counter-example, however, *xhy* 'darken (color)'. Another plausible analysis would be not *xhy* but *khy* since the verb stem *hixha* (verb class 5) is clearly related to *kehe* (adj.: dark). *hixha* would then be analyzed as having undergone spirantization (see previous reference in 2.1.3 and Barkai (1975)).

2.7.2. SPC

The form *hixha* shows that this is not an SPC in the language.

2.7.3. MSSC

The same form also indicates that VGC is not an MSSC since the cluster *xh* arises within the morpheme.

---

[9]VGC is unlike the other constraints (except for /r/ in the SC), inasmuch as there is no homorganic relationship between the consonants in question. Furthermore, while there are constraints which have been discussed in relation to the labial, dental and glottal series, nothing has been said about a "velar constraint". The two points are related. The velar consonants in IH are /k g x/. The stops cannot co-occur because of VC. The origin of many /x/s is a voiceless pharyngeal fricative which subsequently merged with an original velar fricative. Formerly, the pharyngeals and glottals could not co-occur (note Greenberg (1950: 171)). Thus, x and *h*, inter alia, were forbidden in clusters and the original constraint is still reflected in the VGC. The shift of pharyngeal to velar, however, led to the creation of %velar fricative-velar stop sequences at all levels of the grammar, e.g. *lkx* 'take', *xkr* 'lease', *xgg* 'celebrate', *ngx* 'gore', etc.

The reverse *hx* is, of course, not possible as an SPC or as an MSSC because of the phonetic processes which apply to glottal-consonant clusters

VGC, then, is the only sequential constraint applicable at the root level, with no application, either in terms of the word or of the morpheme, at the surface. As such, it reduces the need for sequential constraints to be imposed on the lexical root to near vacuity. One swallow does not make a summer.

3. CONCLUSION

This survey of certain aspects of consonant clustering in IH has led us to the following conclusions:

	CONSTRAINT	STATUS
i)	Identity:	MSSC
ii)	Voicing:	MSSC
iii)	Dental:	no longer viable
iv)	Sonorant:	MSSC
v)	Glottal:	SPC
vi)	Labial:	MSSC
vii)	Velar-Glottal:	? root

To a large extent the findings support Greenberg's claims regarding consonantal sequences in early Semitic. He writes that "these rules [= our constraints: MB] only apply within the morpheme. There is no objection to a sequence of two like consonants when one belongs to another morpheme, e.g. a prefix or a suffix ... the relative absence of patterning in I-III [= R_1 R_3 , MB][10] shows that it is consonants in sequence that are chiefly involved" (1950: 178-9). On the other hand, Greenberg's claim that "they be in close juncture without an intervening vowel does not seem necessary" is not borne out by the modern Hebrew data.

The claim made by Schwarzwald (1975) that these sequential constraints are SPC's is not supported.

That morpheme information is essential to a proper evaluation of the phonological nature of surface words is not surprising in Semitic. We noted in the introduction that, to a large extent, vowels indicate grammatical morphemes (tense or verb class membership, in verbs; to a large extent, derivational morphemes in nouns). Consonants form the lexical framework in which the vowels are embedded. In language-general terms, our findings do not lend support to morpheme structure conditions (note Clayton (1976)) imposed on the consonantal root morpheme. Surface Phonetic constraints imposed on the word may be necessary but are not sufficient for a proper evaluation of the phenomena under discussion. We have endeavoured to show that morphemic information contained within the surface word must be explained in order to arrive at the correct phonotactic generalizations.

[10] Almost completely absent in IH.

REFERENCES

Barkai, M. 1972. "Problems in the phonology of Israeli Hebrew." Doctoral dissertation, University of Illinois, Urbana, Illinois.

Barkai, M. 1975. "On phonological representations, rules and opacity." *Lingua* 37:363-76.

Bolozky, S. 1976. "On the status of fast speech in natural generative phonology." *Proceedings of North-Eastern Linguistic Society* 7:33-46.

Chomsky, N., and M. Halle. 1968. *Sound Pattern of English*. New York: Harper and Row.

Clayton, M.L. 1976. "The redundance of underlying morpheme-structure conditions." *Language* 52:295-313.

Cole, P. 1973. "Mutual bleeding and the ordering of phonological rules." In C.W. Kisseberth (ed.), *Studies in Generative Phonology*, pp. 42-71. Edmonton, Canada: Linguistic Research Inc.

Greenberg, J.H. 1950. "The patterning of root morphemes in Semitic." *Word* 6:162-81.

Halle, M. 1959. *Sound Pattern of Russian*. The Hague: Mouton.

Hooper, J.B. 1975. "The archi-segment in natural generative phonology." *Language* 51:536-60.

Hooper, J.B. 1976. *Introduction to Natural Generative Phonology*. N.Y.: Academic Press.

Hudson, G. 1974. "The role of SPC's in natural generative phonology." *Papers from the Tenth Regional Meeting, Chicago Linguistic Society*, pp. 171-83. Chicago: University of Chicago Department of Linguistics.

Schane, S.A. 1968. *French Morphology and Phonology*. Cambridge, Mass.: M.I.T. Press.

Schwarzwald, O. 1975. "Od beinjan jaxase šoreš vedegem bamilon haivri [More on root-pattern relations in the Hebrew lexicon]." *Hebrew Computational Linguistics* Bulletin No. 9, Bar Ilan University, Israel, pp. 47-59.

Shibatani, M. 1973. "The role of surface phonetic constraints in generative phonology." *Language* 49:87-106.

Ullendorff, E. 1970. "Comparative Semitics." In T.A. Sebeok (ed.), *Current Trends in Linguistics*, vol. 6, pp. 161-73. The Hague: Mouton.

Vennemann, T. 1974. "Words and syllables in natural generative grammar." In a *Parasession on Natural Phonology, Chicago Linguistic Society*, pp. 346-74. Chicago: University of Chicago Department of Linguistics.

Monographic Journals of the Near East *Afroasiatic Linguistics* 6/1 (December 1978)

THE ORDERING OF HEBREW MORPHOLOGICAL PROCESSES

by

Zev Bar-Lev
Ben Gurion University of the Negev, Beersheva, Israel

This article presents a generative analysis of selected aspects of the morphological level in Hebrew, and reveals a complexity of process on this level, involving a mixed ordering of rule-types. It proposes a distinction between syllable-reduplication (as in [kodkod] 'vertex') and consonant-sequence reduplication (as in [bilbel] 'confuse'), and analyzes the distinction as different ordering with respect to vowel-intercalation. It further proposes that the causative prefix /h-/, although an inflectional prefix in syntactic terms, is a root-formative in morphological terms; and that passive /u/ is actually a single, wandering morpheme in three different positions (*pa'ul*, *pu'al*, *hu-ph'al*).

CONTENTS

1. ROOT-FORMATION AND VOWEL-INTERCALATION 16
   1.1. Minor noun reduplication 17
   1.2. Other root-amplification 18

2. VOWEL-INTERCALATION AND STEM-FORMATION 19

   REFERENCES 22

We will propose here that three types of morphological processes in Modern Hebrew (MH) apply in a partly mixed order, namely that the general pattern is the order (1),

(1) a. Root-formation
    b. Vowel-intercalation
    c. Stem-formation

but that individual rules of these types apply in other orders.[1]

---

[1]We are not arguing for extrinsic as opposed to intrinsic ordering. On this point see notes 12 and 13. Our terms "process" and "ordering" could conceivably turn out to have partly metaphorical force, and yet the intricacy that we express here with their help must somehow be captured in any grammar. Aronoff, Jackendoff, and Lightner have revivified morphology as a topic of interest for (modern) linguistics; but their progress seems to be

1. ROOT-FORMATION AND VOWEL-INTERCALATION

Rules of root-formation include various types of amplifications from simple roots, involving either "reduplication" (copying), or "expansion" through addition of root-formatives.

(2) R1. Reduplication of a single consonant, as /dll/ 'dwindle' from /dl-(R1)/, where (R1) is a lexical feature that we assume triggers the reduplication.[2]

R2. Reduplication of a sequence of two consonants, as /blbl/ 'confuse' from /bl-(R2)/.

R3. Reduplication of a whole syllable, as /qodqod/ 'vertex' from /qod-(R3)/.[3]

R4. Root-expansion, by addition of such formatives as /š-, t-, ᵓ-/, as /škpl/ 'duplicate', /tdlq/ 'to fuel', /ᵓkzb/ 'disappoint' from /kpl-(R4')/, /dlq-(R4")/, /kzb-(R4''')/.[4]

---

more in the area of data, since their contribution to a definition of the notion "morphological rule" is somewhat limited. Perhaps the "fault" lies with the languages that they happen to focus on. Investigators of Hebrew who assume (Chayen) or propose (Aronson) a high degree of morphological complexity for this language nevertheless have not succeeded to formulate any of the necessary morphological rules, nor (as we attempt here) to discuss their interaction; investigators of more anti-abstract general orientation (Barkai, Shvartsvald) admit (privately or indirectly) to a morphological complexity for MH that is simply beyond the formalizing capabilites of current linguistics.

[2]We assume that the relationship between /dll/ 'dwindle' and /dl/ 'sparse' is expressed by a lexical rule (see Aronoff, Jackendoff) that relates /dl-(R1)/ and /dl/. In this sense, /dll/ is not derived from the lexical item /dl/, although it is derived from the phonological structure /dl/. Similarly /zmzm/ 'buzz' is phonologically derived from /zm/, but not from any imaginary lexical item */zm/; and /blbl/ 'confuse' is phonologically derived from /bl/, not from the lexical item /bly/ 'wear out' as is traditionally suggested; and /qodqod/ 'vertex' (also 'crown of the head') is phonologically derived from /qod/. The lexical relationship between /qodqod/ in its second meaning and the verb root /qdd/ 'bow one's head' (past /qadad/, etc.) requires the further derivation of /qod/ from /qd/, as is in fact assumed in our further discussion.

[3]Our phonological representation uses certain abstract sounds, mainly the pharyngeals /q,H,9/, along the lines defended in Bar-Lev (MSa).

[4]Compare, with the caveat of note 2, /kpl/ 'double', /dlq/ 'burn', /kzb/ 'lie'. As suggested by our grouping them together, these various root-formatives have similar status in the language today, in spite of differences in origin. All three have "special causative" meaning. It is instructive to note the similarity AND DIFFERENCE from the regular causative CONJUGATION (*hif'il*, with prefix /h-/).

CONJUGATION		ROOT-FORMATION	
/h-Hzr/	'return'(trans.)	/š-Hzr/	'restore'
/h-kpl/	'double'	/š-kpl/	'duplicate (e.g. mimeo)'
/h-gbr/	'strengthen'	/t-gbr/	'reinforce (troops)'
/h-drk/	'lead'	/t-drk/	'give directions'
/h-Hzq/	'hold'	/ᵓ-Hzq/	'maintain (property)'

Our term "special" indicates the presence of some additional semantic feature, e.g. the specific reference to troops in /t-gbr/. This semantic feature is unpredictable, a fact which attests to the derivational status of the root-formation, as does the unpredictability of the specific consonant, as compared with the single consonant /h-/ for the conjugation. Furthermore, the root-formation is conjugated according to the intensive conjugation, while the causative conjugation is independent. In addition, the root-formations are far less

That these are live processes in MH can hardly be doubted: apart from the sheer pervasiveness of obvious instances, they continue to serve as mechanisms for innovations, such as slang [yeke me-yukak] 'yeckefied yecke' ('200% German Jew'), where [me-yukak] 'yeckefied' exhibits a second [k] that can be explained only with reference to R1.

It is rather the distinction between R2 and R3 that is not prima facie obvious. The Semiticist is likely to be as suspicious of R3 as the general inguist is likely to be suspicious of R2. Both these types of readers are likely to be suspicious—for exactly opposite reasons—of the idea of vowel-intercalation, on which our argument will depend. This is not the place for an extensive defense for the existence of particular rule-types,[5] much less for a general consideration of the duality of "Hebrew linguistics". Here we will limit ourselves to brief reference to the justification and indeed formulation of individual rules, and focus on the justification that will come ex post facto, from demonstration of the intricacy of their interaction, which is the proper subject of this paper.

Our task in sections 1.1-1.2, then, will be to show that R3 is indeed different from R2 (and other processes of root-formation), and separated from them by vowel-intercalation.

1.1. MINOR NOUN REDUPLICATION

We begin with the type of reduplication that is formally most straightforward from the point of view of general linguistics, namely syllable reduplication, although, as we will see, this is a much less typical kind of reduplication in MH.

Formally it is not a problem to derive /qodqod/ 'vertex' by whole-syllable duplication, in the terms of note 2, nor even to derive [golgốlet] 'skull' from /gol-(R3)=t/ (where /-t/ is a noun-suffix that is expanded to [-et] by later epenthesis). Convincing indirect evidence for derivation by syllable reduplication is seen in the innovative character of the form [golgốlet] with two [o]'s, as opposed to the older form [gulgốlet].[6]

Direct and compelling motivation for the analysis comes from the exceptional character of the very repetition of the vowel with respect to a deep phonological (morpheme-structure) constraint against multiple non-low vowels:[7] two instances of /o/ (or /u/) cannot occur

---

productive than the conjugation (although even the latter exists for only part of the semantically possible cases). We thus see that the parallel between causative /h-/ and the root-formatives is only partial, and only on certain grammatical levels. (We will later claim that the parallel exists in one further respect, but again without denying the contrast noted here. That is, /h-/ will be proposed to function as a root-formative from the MORPHOLOGICAL point of view, although it is different syntactically and semantically.) On the root-formatives themselves, we may note a difference (apart from relative productivity) in the existence of nouns for expanded roots in /t-, ᵓ-/, such as [tigbốret, tadrix, ᵓaxzaka] 'reinforcements, directions, maintenance'. The existence of these nouns is no doubt a reflection of the origin of the root-formatives /t-, ᵓ-/ from within Hebrew, as opposed to borrowed /š-/, but this difference in origin does not seem to have real significance for the understanding of synchronic relationships. Thus, although these nouns are the historical source for the roots, we would claim that the synchronic relationship between them operates on the root-level, as shown by the difference in their internal vowels and suffixes.

[5]For the defense of the processes themselves, see Bar-Lev (MSb-c).

[6]We should note that the older [gulgolet] also involved syllable reduplication, the deep phonological form being /gulgult/. The innovation here consists simply in making a form more transparent by bringing it out of a process, although that process continues to exist.

[7]See Bar-Lev (1977).

within the boundaries of the root, with the sole exception of these forms.

Now it is obvious that the relevant reduplication rule ("minor noun reduplication", R3) operates on consonant-vowel sequences, rather than on sequences of consonants without vowels. In other words, syllable-reduplication must operate subsequent to any rules of vowel-intercalation.[8]

1.2. OTHER ROOT-AMPLIFICATIONS

But most reduplications in MH involve vowel-patterning of a completely different type, which in fact does not lend itself to analysis in terms of syllable reduplications. For example, /bilbul/ 'confusion' is impossible to derive from /bil/ or /bul/, especially if one must also derive the full variety of verbal forms /bilbel, balbel, bulbal/ (past stem, non-past stem, passive stem) 'to confuse'.

But the more interesting aspect of vowel-patterning regards the placement of vowels with respect to root-consonants, where we seem to observe a "vowel-shift" within the root, between reduplicated and simple forms (in cases where such a pairing exists).[9]

(3)

		/dilul/	'dwindling'
/ᵓišur/	'confirmation'	/ᵓišrur/	'reconfirmation'
		/bilbul/	'confusion'
/kipul/	'doubling'	/šikpul/	'duplication'
/kizub/	'deceit'	/ᵓikzub/	'disappointment'

Of course there are no vowel-shifts here: it is simply that /i/ follows the first root-consonant, and /u/ precedes the last root-consonant—regardless of whether the consonant is original or part of the root-expansion, in both cases.

Expression of this generalization about vowel-placement requires inclusion of the traditional insight of the Hebrew "consonantal root";[10] at the deepest levels, the Hebrew root must be

---

[8]Of course, the existence of vowel-intercalation rules is not proved here, since they are prior to the rules under discussion.

[9]The simple forms here actually contain a medial geminate that we ignore in the presentation and discussion. As a double consonant, this geminate actually provides further instances of the generalization to be proposed.

[10]As discussed in the references in note 5, rules of vowel-intercalation allow natural expression of the whole variety of "intramorphemes" such as /i-u/ "action noun (intensive)", and they explain not only "vowel-shifts" but also "vowel-alternations" of a sort too complex to allow reasonable expression in phonological rules, yet whose productivity is clear in borrowings, such as the following with which we exemplify the alternations.

	'doze'	'neutralize'	'spray'
past	[xarap]	[nitrel]	[hi-špric]
pres.	[xorep]	[me-natrel]	
passive		[me-nutral]	
action n.	[xrip-a]	[nitrul]	[ha-šprac-a]

[xarup], the passive for 'doze', does not exist for syntactic reasons. The two forms of 'spray', [ma-špric, mu-šprac], are omitted because their alternations occur in the prefix rather than within the root. (The forms themselves are of considerable interest for our later discussion.)

a sequence of vowelless consonants, as /dll, ʔšr, ʔšrr, blbl, kpl, škpl, kzb, ʔkzb/, with vowels such as /i-u/ for "verbal noun (intensive)" being introduced into the root from outside by rules of vowel-intercalation.

It is worth emphasizing that the proposed generalization of vowel-placement not only expresses the relationships exemplified in (3), but holds for all vowels in all the verbal forms of these words, even for the longer borrowed root /tlgrf/ 'telegraph' as in /tilgref, talgref, tilgruf/; indeed the generalization holds for the whole language, with a handful of explainable exceptions.[11]

Since the principle of vowel-placement does not distinguish between various kinds of root-amplifications, nor even between amplified roots and simple roots in general, it is clear that vowel-intercalation follows these root-amplifications, namely R1, R2, and R4—although, as shown in section 1.1, it must precede "minor noun reduplication" R3.[12]

2. VOWEL-INTERCALATION AND STEM FORMATION

Under processes of stem-formation we can fairly include the many ordinary phonological processes that affect the shape of stems, e.g. the set of rules that determine the particular vowel in such prefixes as infinitive, future, as exemplified in (4).

(4) [li-sgor, ti-sgor] 'close' (infin., fut.2p.)
[li-xtov, ti-xtov] 'write' (from root /ktb/)
[le-valbel, te-valbel] 'confuse' (root /blbl/)
[le-natrel, te-natrel] 'neutralize'
[la-kum, ta-kum] 'stand up' (root /qm/)

But we are particularly concerned with various rules of quasi-phonological or non-phonological character, that rearrange the underlying structure of words, as exemplified in (5).

(5) a. A rule that deletes the first root-consonant of certain verbs in the infinitive, another rule that adds the infinitive suffix /-t/ for these verbs, e.g. turning /la-hlk/ 'to-go' and /la-yšb/ 'to sit' into /la-lk-t, la-šb-t/, phonetically [laléxet, lašévet].

b. A rule that deletes /-ay/ in verbs such as /qanay/ 'buy' before certain suffixes giving e.g. /qan-u/ 'they bought'), and another rule that changes it to /-i/ before other suffixes (/qani-ti/ 'I bought', rather than */qaney-ti/, cf. the regular phonological development in /bayt-/ 'house-of' → /beyt-/).

c. Rules that (probably in conjunction with the vowel-intercalation rules) give the various arrangements of vowels in stems such as /malk-, mlak-, malak-/ 'king' that will give phonetic [malk-, melax-, malx-].

---

[11]The exceptions involve reduplication and borrowing. We take the position, as originally expressed by Shibatani, that borrowings may not conform to the deepest of phonological principles in the receiver language. For discussion, see Bar-Lev (MSc).

[12]The ordering may, of course, be intrinsic, since the syllable-reduplication rule could refer to syllables with their vowels, and differ in this from R2. A new word such as /gogo/ 'apricot pit' indicates that this must be the case.

(5b) must follow-intercalation, as must all the regular phonological processes involved in stem-formation. (5a) and (5c) are more naturally expressed before intercalation, as we have done here. But there are no compelling arguments that they must do so, so that it is certainly desirable to prove the possibility-in-principle of such an ordering. This we will do by investigating the various wanderings of the passive formative /u/.

Passive /u/ occurs in no less than three different positions, depending on the conjugation (*binyan*).

(6) (a) SIMPLE CONJUGATION: second vowel-position in root

(b) "INTENSIVE" CONJUGATION: first vowel-position in root

(c) CAUSATIVE CONJUGATION: in prefix

Examples:

(a) [sagur] 'closed'

[zaxur] 'remembered'

[katuv] 'written'

(b) [nutral, me-nutral] 'neutralized' (past, pres.)

[bulbal, me-vulbal] 'confused'

[dubar, me-dubar] 'spoken of'

---

[13]Traditionally the simple passive is not regarded as parallel to the other two passives for two reasons: it is defective in its conjugation (lacking tenses as well as infinitive); and there is another passive formation (with prefix /ni-/) that is not defective and can be regarded as simple passive. But for many intensive and causative verbs, the adjectival use of the present is the only form of the passive actually used: *[bulbal, hugzam] 'was confused, was exaggerated'; [mevulbal, mugzam] '(is) confused, exaggerated' (stative, never means 'gets confused, gets exaggerated'). This tendency towards defectiveness is stronger in more colloquial Hebrew, to the extent that the very existence of tenses for these passives could be questioned, i.e. these passives perhaps have completely participial force in the most colloquial Hebrew, and if so they have become parallel to the simple passive in /u/. The following table expresses the relationships between the voices of the two verbs given more accurately than traditional diagrams:

	'write'	'confuse'
active verb:	[katav]	[bilbel]
passive verb:	[ni-xtav]	[hit-balbel]
passive participle:	[katuv]	[me-vulbal]

where [hitbalbel] is the traditional "reflexive", which often, as here, has purely passive meaning. As noted, this table is an accurate statement of relationships for numbers of verbs even in the most formal Hebrew, and has broader application in more colloquial styles. In our exposition, we will not limit ourselves to the most colloquial style of Hebrew, or even to syntactically possible forms: to do so would make the exemplification more complicated, since we want to propose along the way that the causative passive present prefix /mu-/ is in fact a contraction of /m-hu-/, where /hu-/ is the causative passive prefix (itself /h-/+passive /u/), and /m-/ is the present (non-simple) prefix (seen in the intensive as [me-], with transition-vowel [e]). On a more abstract level, then, the forms in table (6) would appear as:

/sagur/
/nutral, m-nutral/
/hu-Hzar, m-hu-Hzar/

(c) [hu-xzar, mu-xzar] 'returned' (root /Hzr/)
[hu-gzam, mu-gzam] 'exaggerated' (root /gzm/)
[hu-šprac, mu-šprac] 'sprayed' (root /šprc/)

One might well doubt the identity of the /u/ in the various positions (especially in view of the defectiveness of (6a) with respect to the tense-system),[13] except that there is direct evidence for their identity in innovative forms in MH. In Classical Hebrew, the passive prefix of (6c) was preferably [ho], obligatorily so with following pharyngeal, e.g. [ho-Hzar]. In MH (although lowering before pharyngeals is probably a live process), the prefix is restored to [hu-] in all cases, with [ho-] as a distinctly formal variant. This restoration of [u] is not explainable except as an attempt to restore phonetic identity to various instances of a single formative, "passive /u/".

The prefix /m-/ of (6b-c), 'pres.', is parallel to the prefixes /l-, t-, .../ 'inf., fut.', exemplified in (4) in the way its vowel is determined; thus [me-valbel] 'confuses' and [me-vulbal] 'is confused' have [e] by virture of the same rules as determine [le-valbel, te valbel] in (4). These rules must operate subsequently to the intercalation of /u/, so as to give [menutral] and not *[muntral].

But it is exactly forms of the latter type that appear in the causative (6c): [mugzam] and not *[meguzam], [huxzar] and not *[hexuzar]. /u/ will be placed correctly in these forms only if the causative prefix is regarded as part of the root for purposes of intercalation, i.e. if /h-/ is regarded as first root-consonant in /hHzr, hgzm, hšprc/.[14]

The causative prefix is thus analyzed, in our present, morphological context, as a formative like those of R4 in (2), a consonantal element added before intercalation. We are NOT claiming that /h-/ belongs to this group of root-formatives in all respects. As we observed in note 4, there are several compelling reasons to maintain the traditional assumption that it belongs to the inflectional system, semantically and syntactically.

Here we are claiming only that in this one morphological respect /h-/ is the first root-consonant. Our argument relates only to the "morphological" level between syntax and phonology, in this case providing the base for vowel-placement. Thus we propose that the distinctive consonant-cluster that seems to begin the root in the causative conjugation, active as well as passive (as in the active causative [he-xzir, hi-gzim, hi-špric] respectively 'return, exaggerate, spray'), is actually just the cluster that gets left in the middle by the principle of vowel-placement, so that the three-consonant cluster of [hušprac] is phonologically parallel to that of [tilgref].

Our various conclusions about ordering of morphological processes can then be summarized as in (8).

(8) a. ROOT-FORMATION:

1. Consonant reduplications (R1, R2)
2. Root expansion (R4), and formation of causative conjugation
3. Morphological rearrangements such as (5a, 5c), /u/-hopping

---

[14]Again, the ordering may be intrinsic, if different types of boundaries are involved. If passive /u/ originates to the right of the consonantal root (as implied by the status of /nutral/, etc. observed in Bar-Lev (1977)), it must be "hopped" to after present-tense /m-/ but before causative /h-/. If causative present /m-/ is analyzed as derived from underlying /m-h-/, as suggested at the end of note 14, then passive /u/ could simply be hopped into between them, and the formulation of rules for vowel-intercalation (Bar-Lev (MSb)) and other rules will do the necessary trick alone.

b. VOWEL-INTERCALATION

c. STEM-FORMATION:

1. Minor noun reduplication (R3)
2. Morphological rearrangements such as (5b)
3. Ordinary phonological processes

(No assumption is made about ordering of 1-2-3 within each group.)

REFERENCES

Aronoff, Mark. 1976. *Word Formation in Generative Grammar*. Cambridge, Mass.: M.I.T. Press.

Aronson, Ruth. 1969. "The predictability of vowel patterns in the Hebrew verb." *Glossa* 3:

Barkai, Malakhi. 1975. "On phonological representations, rules, and opacity." *Lingua* 37:363-76.

Bar-Lev, Zev. 1977. "Migbalot al tnu'ot pnimiyot." *Hebrew Computational Linguistics* no. 12.

Bar-Lev, Zev. MSa. "Natural-abstract Hebrew phonology." To appear in *Folia Linguistica*.

Bar-Lev, Zev. MSb. "Hebrew intramorphemics." To appear in *Linguistics*.

Bar-Lev, Zev. MSc. "The Hebrew morpheme." To appear in *Lingua*.

Chayen, M.J. 1972. "Vowels and transitions in a generative phonology of Israeli Hebrew." *Linguistics* 86:31-40.

Jackendoff, Ray. 1975. "Morphological and semantic regularities in the lexicon." *Language* 51:639-71.

Lightner, Theodore. 1975. "The role of derivational morphology in generative grammar." *Language* 51:617-38.

Shibatani, M. 1973. "The role of surface phonetic constraints in generative phonology." *Language* 49:87-106.

Shvartsvald, Ora. 1973. "Morphological patterns in Hebrew." Doctoral dissertation, University of Texas, Austin.

Skousen, R. 1975. *Substantive Evidence in Phonology*. The Hague: Mouton.

AFROASIATIC DIALECTS

Afroasiatic Dialects (*AAD*) seeks to provide concise descriptions of individual languages which belong to the Afroasiatic language family. It is primarily directed toward an audience consisting, on the one hand, of students of one or several Afroasiatic languages, and, on the other, of students of linguistics. In these volumes, both these groups should find succinct treatises such as to provide familiarity with the basic structure of the language in question in a comparative perspective. Each description will be comprehensive in scope and sufficiently detailed in exemplification. But at the same time the aim will be to cut through to the essential and to avoid specialized argumentation. The goal then is neither to publish a corpus of exhaustive reference grammars nor to provide a platform for the analytical defense of theoretical questions. In this sense the series is properly data-oriented. Though the authors will necessarily be of a variety of theoretical persuasions and each will have his own set of preferences for presentation, not the least important goal will be to achieve as high a degree as possible of uniformity in structure, and in the conventional signs and terminology used. This being accomplished, the reader should have no difficulty in finding points of resemblance and divergence amongst the languages which concern him with regard to some point of inquiry. The term 'dialects' in the series' title refers not only to modern spoken vernaculars but to historically definable stages of any language of the various branches. Publication of studies of as many such dialects as possible would provide, we feel, both an encouragement to comparative work and a sound documentary base on which alone this work may fruitfully progress.

AAD 1 - **Berber:** *TAMAZIGHT OF THE AYT NDHIR* by Thomas G. Penchoen. 1973, IV-124 pp., $8.50.

The Ayt Ndhir dialect which is described belongs to one of the major Berber languages, Tamazight, spoken in the Middle Atlas Mountains of central Morocco. The description is based in the main on research undertaken with native speakers of the Ayt Ndhir territory surrounding El Hajeb. – While directed to the non-specialist, a number of points in the description proper will be of interest to the specialist as well: the presentation of noun and verb morphology points up a number of regularities which more often than not have been obscured in previous descriptions. Also, phonological rules are given which account for the major share of morphophonemic complexities. The reader will find in the appendices and 'optional' sections conjugation tables of typical verbs–including detailed observations on the placement of shwa in verbs–, a chart showing the main morphological patterns involved in verb derivation, a description of the phonological rules applying in complex sequences of morphemes of the verb group, the 'basic' vocabulary contained in several well-known lexicostatistic word lists, and a chart of the Tifinaγ alphabet used by the Tuareg.

AAD 2 - **Ancient Egyptian:** *MIDDLE EGYPTIAN* by John Callender. 1975, 150 pp., $10.

This grammar deals with the literary language used in Egypt from ca. 2000 to 1200 B.C. and considered in even later times to be the classical written form of Egyptian. The book is directed toward the general linguist as well as the Egyptologist; examples are glossed and written in transcription and there is an index of grammatical terms and Egyptian morphemes. A comprehensive set of paradigms of both verbal and non-verbal predicate types is included as an appendix, together with an appendix on negation and one on the historical origin of certain constructions. – The grammar contains three main parts: phonology, morphology, and syntax, of which the last receives most emphasis. The section on phonology sketches the laws of sound change to the extent they can be discovered. The section on morphology stresses the paradigmatic character of verb tenses and their derivations. A distinction is made between truly paradigmatic tenses and tenses borrowed from Old Egyptian for quotations or special effect. Following Polotsky, the "emphatic forms" are treated as nominalizations under the rubric "manner nominalizations." Unlike previous grammars of Egyptian, this grammar discusses syntax according to transformational categories. The process of "clefting" interrelates emphatic forms, the "participial statement" and constructions with *pw+* relatives. The process character of negation is emphasized, and the implications of so considering it are developed in a special appendix. A sample text is also included, accompanied by a vocabulary and a translation.

AAD 3 - **Semitic:** *DAMASCUS ARABIC* by Arne Ambros. 1977, vii-123 pp., $13.

Based on both previous works and the author's own observations, the grammar describes the Sedentary Eastern Arabic dialect spoken in Damascus. While strictly synchronic and written without presupposing knowledge of classical Arabic, it follows traditional arrangement and terminology as closely as possible without failing however to do justice to the individual traits of the dialect. Appendices deal with 1) the regular reflexes of Classical Arabic phonemes in Damascus Arabic, and rules governing the reduction of vowels, and 2) a discussion of morphological substitutions which cannot be interpreted as describing the historical development from Classical Arabic to Damascus Arabic.

All prices are postpaid. Payment must accompany orders from individuals. A handling fee of $1.00 will be charged to libraries if order is not prepaid. Discount of 20% on all orders received within one year of publication date.
Order from: UNDENA PUBLICATIONS, P.O. Box 97, Malibu, California 90265, U.S.A.

SOURCES AND MONOGRAPHS ON THE ANCIENT NEAR EAST

Editors: Giorgio Buccellati, Marilyn Kelly-Buccellati, Piotr Michalowski

These two series make available original documents in English translation (Sources) and important studies by modern scholars (Monographs) as a contribution to the study of history, religion, literature, art and archaeology of the Ancient Near East. Inexpensive and flexible in format, they are meant to serve the specialist by bringing within easy reach basic publications often in updated versions, to provide imaginative educational outlets for undergraduate and graduate courses, and to reach the interested segments of the educated lay audience.

SOURCES FROM THE ANCIENT NEAR EAST

Volume One

Fascicle 1: R. I. Caplice, *The Akkadian Namburbi Texts: An Introduction.* 24 pp., $2.00.

Fascicle 2: M. E. Cohen, *Balag-Compositions: Sumerian Lamentation Liturgies of the Second and First Millennium B.C.* 34 pp., $2.85.

Fascicle 3: Luigi Cagni, *The Poem of Erra.* 62 pp., $5.20.

Fascicle 4: Gary Beckman, *Hittite Birth Rituals: An Introduction.* 21 pp., $1.75.

Fascicle 5: S. M. Burstein, *The* Babyloniaca *of Berossus.* 39 pp., $3.30.

MONOGRAPHS ON THE ANCIENT NEAR EAST

Volume One

Fascicle 1: A. Falkenstein, *The Sumerian Temple City* (1954). Introduction and Translation by M. DeJ. Ellis. 21 pp., $1.85.

Fascicle 2: B. Landsberger, *Three Essays on the Sumerians* (1943-45). Introduction and Translation by M. DeJ. Ellis. 18 pp., $1.50.

Fascicle 3: I. M. Diakonoff, *Structure of Society and State in Early Dynastic Sumer* (1959). Summary and Translation of selected passages by the author. Introduction by M. Desrochers. 16 pp., $1.35.

Fascicle 4: B. Landsberger, *The Conceptual Autonomy of the Babylonian World* (1926). Translation by Th. Jacobsen, B. Foster and H. von Siebenthal. Introduction by Th. Jacobsen. 16 pp., $1.35.
